POTATOES

Tasty and easy to make recipes

Nayna Kanabar

Health Harmony

An imprint of

B. Jain Publishers (P) Ltd.
USA — Europe — India

Preface

Cooking is something I started doing at a very young age. I cooked my first meal at the age of 10 for my unsuspecting 15 year old brother when we were home alone whilst our parents were out for the day. My mother was my inspiration; I would watch her meticulously prepare elaborate meals to satisfy my father's enjoyment and passion for food and feed the numerous visitors that always appeared on our doorstep and never left without a meal. In our home we consumed mainly vegetarian Gujarati food, however after immigrating to the United Kingdom, I was introduced to western flavours. This is where my passion for cooking brought me to sample fusion and multinational cuisines.

My real enthusiasm for cooking finally emerged when I married and had a family of my own. My kitchen was my own work space; the ingredients were my tools and here I explored new flavours and textures and experimented with Asian and international cuisines. I soon realised I needed somewhere to share my recipes and so my food blog **Simply Food** was set up. I cook, photograph and post recipes created in my kitchen on a regular basis on my blog. From the blog an idea emerged to write a book where the focus would be one main ingredient. As my daughter was going through a phase where she would only eat a dish that had some form of potato in it, I rose to the challenge and started creating a series of recipes using potatoes as a main ingredient and the book **Potatoes** was born.

I experimented with every day recipes and developed them into new by introducing new flavours and removing some. Some dishes turned out wonderful and others just did not work or satisfy our palates. My main critics throughout all these experiments have been my husband and two daughters who have been my panel of judges and it is through them that I have selected the best 50 potato recipes to share in this book.

Publisher's Note

Potato is a widely eaten vegetable that comes in a variety of avatars. It can be baked, fried, boiled as a whole or more than often is consumed as an accompaniment to other vegetables. Potatoes, despite their status, are a good way to stay healthy and are very nutritious.

Nayna Kanabar is an accomplished cook and an author who has spiced up the 'simple' home cooking. In 'Potatoes', she has brought forth a fabulous assortment of mouth-watering dishes made using Potato as the chief ingredient. Her passion for cooking introduced her to a variety of cuisines. It was in her kitchen that she explored varying and contrasting flavours, and textures of food.

We are extremely pleased to present this extraordinary book called Potatoes, which is not just another recipe book but is a whole new approach to cook Potatoes and explore the varying tastes which this humble vegetable holds.

- Kuldeep Jain, CEO

Contents

Morrocan / African Cuisine

- Lentil and Potato Soup 7
- Honey Sweet Potatoes 8
- Sweet Potato and Apple Phyllo Parcels 9
- Vegetable Kebabs... 10
- Sweet Potato and Date Halwa...................................... 12
- Potato, Peanut and Sweet Corn Hotpot.....................13

Spanish Cuisine

- Hasselback Roast Potatoes... 14
- Canarian Potatoes with Mojo Sauce 15
- Potato Frittata 16

European Cuisine

- Sweet Potato and Tomato Soup 17
- New Herb Potatoes...18
- Mediterranean Vegetable and Potato Stew 19
- Potato Sushi Rolls 20
- Sweet Potato and Red Cabbage Stir Fry 22

British Cuisine

- Potato Fries... 23
- Potato and Vegetable Pie 24
- Sweet Potato Crisps.. 26

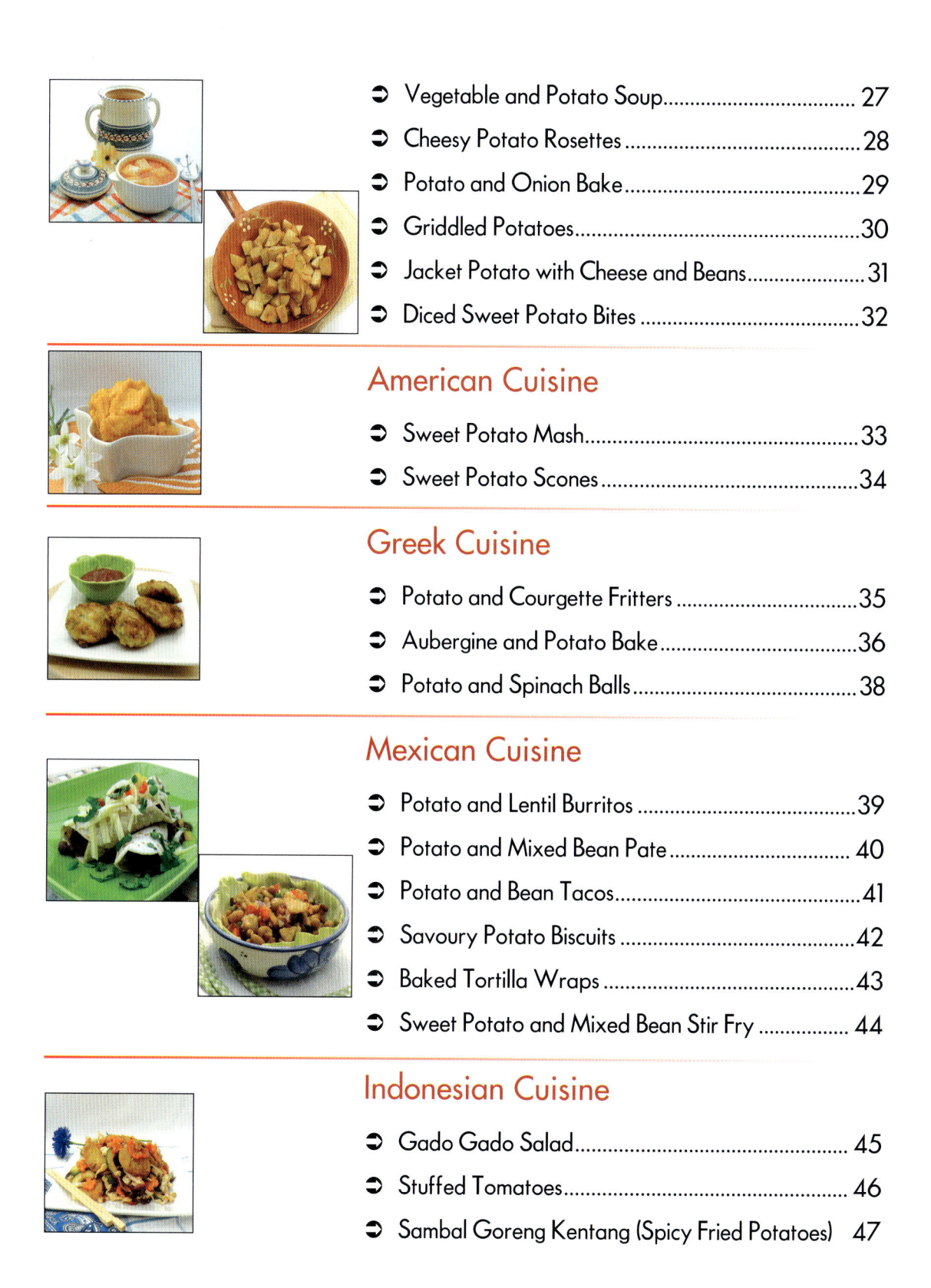

- Vegetable and Potato Soup 27
- Cheesy Potato Rosettes 28
- Potato and Onion Bake 29
- Griddled Potatoes 30
- Jacket Potato with Cheese and Beans 31
- Diced Sweet Potato Bites 32

American Cuisine

- Sweet Potato Mash 33
- Sweet Potato Scones 34

Greek Cuisine

- Potato and Courgette Fritters 35
- Aubergine and Potato Bake 36
- Potato and Spinach Balls 38

Mexican Cuisine

- Potato and Lentil Burritos 39
- Potato and Mixed Bean Pate 40
- Potato and Bean Tacos 41
- Savoury Potato Biscuits 42
- Baked Tortilla Wraps 43
- Sweet Potato and Mixed Bean Stir Fry 44

Indonesian Cuisine

- Gado Gado Salad 45
- Stuffed Tomatoes 46
- Sambal Goreng Kentang (Spicy Fried Potatoes) 47

Asian Fusion Cuisine

- Sesame Coins 48
- Bread Appetizers 49
- Spicy Potato Nests 50
- Spicy Potato Croquettes 52
- Potato and Lentil Pancakes 53

Indo Chinese Cuisine

- Spring Rolls 54
- Potato and Vegetable Stir Fry 56
- Sweet and Sour Potatoes 57

Indian Cuisine

- Potato and Peas Curry 58
- Sweet Potato Pudding 59
- Baby Potatoes in White Gravy 60
- Egg and Potato Curry 61
- Bombay Potatoes 62

INDEX 64

Preparation time
10 minutes

Soaking time
overnight

Cooking time
40 minutes

Serves
4

Lentil and Potato Soup

Ingredients

120 g / 4 oz Dried green lentils
2 Medium potatoes peeled and diced
2 Medium tomatoes deseeded and finely chopped
1 Small finely diced onion

2 tablespoons Olive oil
2 Green chillies finely minced
1 Clove of garlic finely minced
1 litre Water

1 teaspoon Corn flour
1 ½ teaspoons Salt
½ teaspoon White pepper powder
½ teaspoon Cumin powder

Method

- Wash and soak the lentils overnight.
- In a pressure cooker place the lentils with the water and cook till tender.
- In a large pan add the oil and sauté the onions and garlic till soft and translucent.
- Add the potato and the tomatoes and the cooked lentils and bring them to boil, reduce heat and simmer for 10 minutes till potato is cooked.
- Mix the corn flour with 1 tablespoon water and add to the soup. Simmer for 2-3 minutes more to thicken the soup.
- Season with cumin powder, salt and pepper and chillies. Adjust seasoning as required.

Serve with bread and butter.

Rich and spicy potato and lentil soup full of protein with a hot spicy kick.

Preparation time
30 minutes

Cooking time
20 minutes

Serves
2

Honey Sweet Potatoes

Ingredients

1 Medium sweet potato
½ Red pepper
½ Green pepper
1 Bowl shredded ice berg lettuce

2 tablespoons Orange juice
1 tablespoon Lemon juice
½ teaspoon Salt
½ teaspoon Fresh ground black pepper

1 tablespoon Honey
½ tablespoon Butter

Method

- Boil the sweet potato in its skin.
- Cool the boiled sweet potato, remove skin and dice into 1 cm pieces.
- Finely dice the red and green peppers.
- In a frying pan heat the butter and add the lemon juice, orange juice and honey. When it starts to simmer add the diced potatoes and simmer until orange juice and honey sauce reduces and coats the pototoes.
- Add the diced peppers to the potatoes and season with salt and pepper. Gently toss the honey potatoes.
- Line a serving dish with the shredded lettuce and top with honey sweet potatoes.

Serve hot with Frittata.

Sweet potatoes laced with sweet honey and citrus glaze.

Potatoes – Morrocan / African Cuisine

Preparation time
30 minutes

Cooking time
20 minutes

Serves
4

Sweet Potato and Apple Phyllo Parcels

Ingredients

8 Sheets phyllo pastry (dimension 9 inch x 9 inch)
60 g / 2 oz Melted butter
1 Medium gala apple
1 Medium sweet potato
½ teaspoon Cinnamon powder
30 g / 1 oz Raisins
1 tablespoon Lemon juice
2 tablespoons Brown sugar
15 g / ½ oz Almond flakes
Icing sugar for dusting

Method

- Core the apple and dice it into small pieces. Place it in a bowl and add lemon juice to it.
- Boil the sweet potato until it is tender but not over cooked.
- Peel and dice the potato in small pieces and add it to the apples.
- Add cinnamon, brown sugar, almonds and raisins and toss the filling to coat the apple and sweet potato with sugar and spice.
- On a flat surface lay a sheet of phyllo pastry and brush it with melted butter. Place a second sheet of phyllo on top of the buttered sheet and brush with more butter.
- Spoon a quarter of the potato and apple mixture in the centre of the pastry square and gather up all 4 corners to form a little parcel.
- Gently apply pressure and twist so that the pastry parcels holds together and the pastry corners fan out.
- Repeat the process for remaining sheets of pastry.
- Grease a baking tray and place the parcels on it. Bake in a preheated oven 175°C / 350°F for about 15-20 minutes or until the pastry starts to get crisp and browns slightly.
- Remove from the oven and place on a serving dish. Dust with Icing sugar and garnish with few raisins and almond slices.

Serve immediately.

Cinnamon scented sweet potato and apple filling in crispy thin pastry.

Potatoes – Morrocan / African Cuisine

Preparation time	Cooking time	Chilling time	Serves
30 minutes	30 minutes	30 minutes	4

Vegetable Kebabs

Ingredients

2 Medium boiled potatoes
1 Carrot
120 g / 4 oz Peas
120 g / 4 oz Sweet corn

2 Green chillies finely chopped
1 teaspoon Salt
½ teaspoon Turmeric powder
½ teaspoon Chilli powder

½ teaspoon Garam masala
1 tablespoon Lemon juice
1 tablespoon Chilli sauce
2 Teaspoons Corn flour

4 tablespoons Bread crumbs
2 tablespoons Breadcrumbs for final coating for kebabs
2 tablespoon Sunflower oil for cooking

NB- Garam masala- coriander seeds, cumin seeds, black pepper corns, black cumin seeds, dry ginger powder, cardamom, cloves, cinnamon.

Method

- Soak some wooden skewers in water.
- Grate the potatoes.
- Coarsely grind the peas and sweet corn.
- Peel and grate carrot.
- In a pan heat one tablespoon of oil, add carrots, peas and sweet corn.
- Stir fry for 6-8 minutes till cooked. Add the cooked grated potatoes and mix well.
- Add salt, chillies, turmeric, and chilli powder, garam masala, chilli sauce and lemon juice and stir fry for 2 more minutes.
- Cool the mixture and once cooled, add the corn flour and bread crumbs and mix it to form a stiff mixture. Divide the mixture into 8 parts and roll each part into a sausage shape approx 5 inches long.
- In a shallow dish place the remaining bread crumbs, roll the sausages in the breadcrumbs to coat them and then place them on a tray. Cover and place in the refrigerator to chill for 30 minutes.
- After 30 minutes remove from refrigerator and gently push a soaked wooden skewer into each sausage and spray a little cooking oil over each kebab.
- Place the skewers under a hot grill or on a barbecue to cook, rotate the skewers to ensure even cooking. Kebabs are ready when they turn golden brown. (It will take approximately 7-10 minutes)

Serve hot on a bed of Rice with some mint Chutney.

Fresh vegetables cooked and flavoured in a blend of mild aromatic spices and encased in breadcrumbs and grilled on skewers.

Preparation time
10 minutes

Cooking time
15 minutes

Chilling time
30 minutes

Serves
4

Sweet Potato and Date Halwa

Ingredients

240g / 8 oz Boiled sweet potato puree
30 g / 1 oz Butter
30 g / 1 oz Milk powder
30 ml Coconut milk

3 tablespoons Powdered sugar
1 teaspoon Cardamom powder
½ teaspoon Rose water
Few strands of saffron

60g / 2 oz Fresh grated coconut
6 Ripe dates finely chopped
6 Ripe dates stoned and cut in halves

Method

- In a pan heat the butter, when it has melted, add sweet potato puree and coconut milk and cook until the mixture thickens. Keep stirring to avoid it sticking to the bottom of the pan. (Approximately 5 minutes)
- Add chopped dates and powdered milk and cook until the raw smell of the powdered milk is gone. (Approximately 4-5 minutes)
- Remove the halwa from the heat and allow it to cool slightly.
- Once the halwa is slightly cooled, add powdered sugar, cardamom powder, saffron and rose water and mix well.
- Grease a shallow dish with some melted butter and put the halwa into the dish. Smooth it using the back of a spoon until it is well packed into the dish.
- Dry roast the grated coconut in dry frying pan for 1-2 minutes.
- Sprinkle the coconut on top of the halwa and pat it smooth with a spoon.
- Decorate the top of the halwa with the date halves.

Serve this warm or chilled.

Aromatic Middle Eastern flavours of cardamom, saffron and rose water makes this dessert simply divine.

12 | Potatoes – Morrocan / African Cuisine

Preparation time
15 minutes

Cooking time
30 minutes

Serves
4

Potato, Peanut and Sweet Corn Hotpot

Ingredients

180 g / 6 oz Diced boiled potatoes
4 Whole boiled Corn on the Cob
1 Medium onion finely diced
1 teaspoon Garlic paste
1 teaspoon Ginger paste

2-3 Bay leaves
2 teaspoons Salt
1 teaspoon Turmeric
1 teaspoon Coriander powder
1 teaspoon Cumin powder

60 g /2 oz Peanuts coarsely ground
1/2 cup Coconut milk
3 green Chillies finely chopped
2 tablespoon Sunflower oil

1 tablespoon Tomato puree
1 teaspoon Chilli powder

Method

- Using a sharp knife remove the corn kernels from two boiled whole corns. Keep them aside.
- Cut the other two corns into 1 cm thick slices. Keep them aside.
- In a pan heat the oil. When it is hot, add bay leaves, ginger and garlic paste and the onions and sauté until translucent.
- Add the tomato puree, green chillies, salt, chilli powder, cumin powder, coriander powder, turmeric and cook until all the spices have infused.
- Add the coarsely ground peanuts and sauté for further 2-3 minutes.
- Add 150 ml water, potatoes, corn slices and corn kernels to the sauce and simmer on a low heat for 10 minutes.
- Add coconut milk and simmer for another 5 minutes. Add a little extra water if the gravy is too thick.

Transfer to serving dish and garnish with chopped fresh coriander. Serve with pitta bread.

Corn the cob cut into bite sized discs, cooked with an array of aromatic spices in a rich and spicy peanut and coconut gravy.

Preparation time
15 minutes

Cooking time
40 minutes

Serves
4

Hasselback Roast Potatoes

Ingredients

16 Baby new potatoes, washed

1 teaspoon Coarse sea salt

2 tablespoons Olive oil

1 teaspoon Coarsely ground black pepper

1 teaspoon Garlic paste

Method

- Wash the potatoes and keep the skin on.
- Place the potato on a chopping board and cut slices ¾ of the way into each potato every 5 mm part, make sure that the potato is not sliced all the way through to the base. The idea is to have 7-8 slices of potatoes all still stuck together at the base which will fan out during roasting.
- Mix the garlic paste with the oil and rub the garlic oil all over the potatoes.
- Place the potatoes on an oiled baking tray.
- Season with coarsely ground black pepper and sea salt and bake the potatoes in a preheated oven at 200°C / 400°F for 40-45 minutes till potatoes turn crisp and golden brown and are cooked through. The potato slices will separate and fan open during cooking.

Serve as a side dish to a main meal.

Crispy oven roasted baby new potatoes in jackets with a spicy seasoned coating.

Preparation time
5 minutes

Cooking time
30 minutes

Serves
4

Canarian Potatoes with Mojo Sauce

Ingredients

20 Small white baby potatoes
900 m / 1 ½ Pints water
4 tablespoons Rock salt
1 teaspoon Coarsely grounded black pepper

Mojo sauce ingredients
1 long Red pepper
½ teaspoon Salt
4 Cloves and garlic
3 red Hot chillies
3 tablespoons Olive oil

Method

Mojo Sauce:
- Remove the seeds and membrane from both the pepper and red chillies and chop them coarsely.
- Peel the garlic.
- Add pepper, chillies, salt, olive oil and garlic to a blender and grind to form a smooth paste.
- Transfer to a serving dish.

Potatoes:
- Wash the potatoes and place them in a saucepan with the water. Add all the salt.
- Bring the potatoes to a boil and cook for 20 minutes till they are tender.
- Drain most of the access liquid from the potatoes but leave a small amount in the bottom of the pan.
- Return the pan with the potatoes and small amount of cooking water and cook the potatoes until the remaining water evaporates. Stir the potatoes around till they dry up and skins start to crisp up. You see a white salt coating forming on the potatoes.
- Transfer the potatoes to a serving dish and sprinkle with some coarsely grounded pepper.

Serve with Mojo Sauce.

Small baby potatoes cooked in their jackets with a rock crusty salt coating.

Preparation time
5 minutes

Cooking time
15 minutes

Serves
2

Potato Frittata

Ingredients

4 Eggs
2 Small boiled potatoes
1 Bowl precooked mixed vegetables (sweet corn/peas/green beans/carrots)
1 Small red onion finely diced
2 Small button mushrooms finely diced
1 teaspoon Salt
½ teaspoon White pepper powder
½ teaspoon Chilli flakes
30 ml Milk
2 tablespoons Olive oil

Method

- Slice the potatoes into thin round slices and keep them aside.
- In a bowl break the eggs, add milk, salt, pepper, chilli flakes and beat them together.
- Add 1 tablespoon oil to the frying pan, when it is hot add chopped onions to it and sauté till translucent. Add precooked vegetables and mushrooms and sauté for 2-3 more minutes.
- Add the beaten eggs to the mixed vegetables and cook the eggs till they just start to set.
- Place the sliced potatoes on top of the partly cooked egg mixture and season with salt and pepper.
- Drizzle the potato slices with remaining oil. Remove the frying pan from the cooker and place it under a hot grill to set the top of the frittata.
- Once eggs have set and the potato starts to brown slightly, remove the frittata from the grill.
- Cut the frittata into wedges and serve them hot.

Serve with toast for breakfast or salad for lunch.

Delicious and wholesome brunch dish that is healthy and filling.

16 | Potatoes – Spanish Cuisine

Preparation time
10 minutes

Cooking time
30 minutes

Serves
4

Sweet Potato and Tomato Soup

Ingredients

1 Medium sweet potato diced
1 Medium carrot diced
8 Tomatoes diced
2 Cups water
1 Bay leaf
½ teaspoon Black pepper
1 teaspoon Salt
½ teaspoon Sugar

Method

- Blend the tomatoes in a blender jug and puree them. Strain to remove skin and seeds and pour them into a saucepan and simmer on medium heat.
- Add the bay leaf to the potato and carrots and pressure cook them with 1 cup water.
- Once vegetables are cooked remove the bay leaf and add them to the simmering tomato puree.
- Add more water to get desired consistency. Add salt, pepper and sugar. Taste and adjust seasoning as required. Simmer for 5 more minutes.
- You can either puree the soup in a blender jug to make it smooth or leave it chunky.
- Transfer to a serving bowl and serve hot with fresh bread.

Tangy and delicious soup that is fast and speedy to make.

Preparation time
5 minutes

Cooking time
20 minutes

Serves
4

New Herb Potatoes

Ingredients

- 480 g / 16 oz Baby new potatoes
- 30 g / 1oz Salted butter
- 1 tablespoon Fresh finely chopped parsley
- ½ tablespoon Fresh chopped chives
- ½ teaspoon Salt
- ½ teaspoon Ground black pepper

Method

- Wash and steam the potatoes in their jackets till tender.
- Place the hot cooked potatoes in a bowl, add half the butter, add the chopped parsley and chives and season with salt and pepper.
- Toss the potatoes and cover and leave for 2-3 minutes for flavours to infuse.
- Transfer the potatoes to a serving dish and add the remaining butter on the top.

Serve as side dish to compliment any main course.

New baby potatoes steamed in their jackets and tossed in herb and butter dressing.

Potatoes – European Cuisine

Preparation time
15 minutes

Cooking time
35 minutes

Serves
4

Mediterranean Vegetable and Potato Stew

Ingredients

60 g / 2 oz Pre cooked sweet corn kernels
60 g / 2 oz Mixed peppers diced
60 g / 2 oz Green beans finely chopped
120 g / 4 oz Mixed precooked beans borlotti/ aduki /cannellini beans

2 Medium potatoes finely diced
1 Small onion finely diced
60 g / 2 oz Courgettes finely diced
120 g / 4 oz Baked beans in tomato sauce
4 Medium tomatoes finely chopped

1 teaspoon Salt
2 teaspoons Dried Italian spice (oregano)
½ teaspoon Black pepper
2 Chillies finely chopped
1 teaspoon Garlic paste
1 tablespoon Olive oil

Method

- In a pan heat the oil when it is hot, add the onions and garlic. Sauté till translucent. Add the tomatoes and cook till tomatoes soften and break up.
- Add peppers, sweet corn, courgettes, green beans, mixed beans and potatoes. Add 150 ml water and simmer the stew until the potatoes are soft and tender.
- Add salt, pepper, chillies and baked beans and continue to simmer on a low heat. Add a little more water if needed.
- Add the Italian spice, stir it into the stew and remove from heat. Transfer the stew to a serving bowl.

Serve with garlic bread and side salad.

Hearty, nutritious and wholesome one pot meal.

Potatoes – European Cuisine

Preparation time
30 minutes

Serves
4

Potato Sushi Rolls

Ingredients

Filling 1
1 large long cucumber
1 Medium boiled potato
1 tablespoon Tomato puree
½ teaspoon Chilli flakes

½ teaspoon Salt
1 tablespoon Lemon juice
1 Carrot

Filling 2
1 Medium boiled potato

1 tablespoon Pickled jalapeños
18 Green olives
½ teaspoon Salt
½ teaspoon White pepper
1 tablespoon Lemon juice

Method

- Cut the ends of the cucumber and slice lengthways the top thin slice and discard it. Continue to slice the cucumber lengthways into long paper thin strips using a mandolin and discard the very last slice too.
- For filling 1, mash the boiled potato and put it into a bowl, add tomato puree, chilli flakes, salt and lemon juice and mix well.
- Grate the carrot and keep it aside.
- To roll the sushi, place two long strips of cucumber one on top of the other.
- Spread a very thin layer of the potato filling 1 on top of the cucumber strip.
- Starting at one end, leaving approximately 1 cm gap place a small bunch of grated carrot on top of the potato filling at that end.
- Start rolling the cucumber strip tightly from the end where the carrot is placed and continue rolling it to the other end.
- Place the rolled sushi rolls onto a serving platter. Repeat for remainder of the filling.
- For filling 2, mash the potato and put it into a bowl.
- Finely chop 6 olives and add it to the mashed potato.
- Finely chop the jalapeños and add to the potatoes.
- Add salt, pepper and lemon juice and mix well.
- To roll the sushi, place two long strips of cucumber one on top of the other.
- Spread a very thin layer of the potato filling 2 on top of the cucumber strip.
- Starting at one end, leaving approximately 1 cm gap place 2 olives at this end.
- Start rolling the cucumber strip tightly from the end where the olives are placed and continue rolling it to the other end.
- Place rolled sushi onto a serving platter. Repeat for remainder of the filling.

Serve immediately with a hot chilli oil dip.

Paper thin cucumber with tangy potato filling served with hot chilli oil dip.

Preparation time
10 minutes

Cooking time
10 minutes

Serves
2

Sweet Potato and Red Cabbage Stir Fry

Ingredients

1 Medium sweet potato

120 g / 4 oz Shredded red cabbage

1 tablespoon White wine vinegar

½ teaspoon Salt

½ teaspoon Paprika powder

1 tablespoon Olive oil

Method

- Peel and dice the sweet potato.
- In a wok, heat the oil when it is hot add the diced potato and cabbage and stir fry for 10 minutes until potatoes are tender and cooked and cabbage has wilted.
- Add salt, paprika and white wine vinegar and mix well.
- Transfer to a serving dish.

Serve hot as an accompaniment to any main course.

Sweet tasting potato with a crunchy cabbage in a tangy tantalising stir fry.

22 | Potatoes – European Cuisine

Preparation time
10 minutes

Cooking time
20 minutes

Serves
2

Potato Fries

Ingredients

3 Large potatoes

900 ml Sunflower oil for deep frying

¼ teaspoon Salt

¼ teaspoon Pepper

Method

- Peel the potatoes and wash them.
- Dry the potatoes and slice them into thin fries.
- Heat oil in a deep pan, when oil is hot deep fry the potato fries on medium heat until golden brown and crispy.
- Remove from oil and drain on kitchen paper.
- Sprinkle with salt and pepper and serve with tomato ketchup.

Thin potato fries, deep fried till golden brown and crispy. A tasty and delectable snack.

Preparation time	Cooking time	Chilling time	Serves
40 minutes	45 minutes	30 minutes	4

Potato and Vegetable Pie

Ingredients

480 g / 16 oz Small boiled potatoes
240 g / 8 oz Pre cooked mixed kidney beans
240 g / 8 oz Diced seasonal mixed vegetables (peas/ carrots/ french beans/ mushrooms)
1 Medium onion finely diced
1 ½ teaspoons Salt
1 teaspoon Black pepper
240 g / 8 oz Tinned chopped plum tomatoes
2 tablespoons Tomato ketchup
1 tablespoon Oregano
2 tablespoons Olive oil

For pastry:
240 g / 8 oz Plain flour
4 oz Chilled butter
½ teaspoon Salt
4-6 tablespoons Iced water

Method

Pastry:

- Sieve the flour and salt together in a bowl and add to a food processor.
- Cut the butter into 1 cm cubes and add to the food processor with the flour.
- Pulse the flour and butter for 1 minute until a texture resembling bread crumbs forms.
- Add iced water a little at a time until pastry forms into a ball.
- Remove from food processor and wrap in cling film. Do not knead it or handle it too much.
- Chill for 30 minutes.

Filling:

- In a pan add the oil and when it is hot add the onions. Sauté them until they turn translucent.
- Add the tinned tomatoes together with the juice, beans and vegetables. Add tomato ketchup.
- Season with salt, pepper, oregano and simmer the mixture until it thickens.
- Remove from heat and allow it to cool.
- Slice the potato into 5 mm thick slices and keep them aside.
- Take the pastry out of the refrigerator and on a floured surface roll out a circle large enough to line an ovenproof pie dish. Pastry thickness should be approximately 5 mm thick.
- Transfer the rolled pastry to the pie dish and smooth it into the dish covering bottom and sides of dish. Cut off excess pastry on the rim of the pie dish with a sharp knife. Prick the base and sides of the pastry with a fork.
- Preheat an oven to 175°C / 350°F. Blind bake the empty pie shell for 15 minutes till it turns golden brown.
- Remove the baked pastry shell from the oven and fill it with the prepared filling.
- Place the potato slices on top of the bean filling and season with salt and pepper. Brush them with a little oil and return the pie to the oven to be baked for another 25-30 minutes.
- Remove pie from oven and allow it to cool slightly before serving.

Serve with fresh garden salad.

NB-Blind bake means to bake a pie crust without a filling, to brown it first.

Melt in the mouth short crust pastry with a nutritious vegetable and tomato filling with a wonderful potato crust.

Preparation time
20 minutes

Cooking time
20 minutes

Serves
2

Sweet Potato Crisps

Ingredients

1 Large sweet potato

900 ml Sunflower oil

3 tablespoons Chilli dip for serving

Method

- Peel the sweet potato and slice it very thinly using a mandolin.
- Wash the potato slices and pat them dry on a tea towel.
- Ensure that the slices are completely dry and separate them.
- In a wok add oil and heat it.
- When oil is hot, drop small handful of potato slices in hot oil and fry on medium heat until crisp.
- Drain on kitchen paper.
- Transfer to a serving dish.

Serve with Chilli dip.

Crunchy and delectable crisps that are perfect for party nibbles.

Preparation time
15 minutes

Cooking time
30 minutes

Serves
4

Vegetable and Potato Soup

Ingredients

- 2 Medium potatoes peeled and diced
- 2 Medium carrots peeled and diced
- 2 Sticks celery cleaned and diced
- 1 Green pepper diced
- 1 Red pepper diced
- 4 Medium tomatoes deseeded and finely chopped
- 1 Small red onion finely chopped
- 2 tablespoons Olive oil
- 1 Clove of garlic finely minced
- 1 teaspoon Dried oregano
- 900 ml Water
- 1½ teaspoons Salt
- ½ teaspoon Paprika powder
- Bread croutons for garnishing

Method

- In a large pan, add oil and sauté the onions and garlic till soft and translucent.
- Add potato, celery, peppers, carrots and tomatoes and sauté for another 3-4 minutes. Add water and bring it to boil, reduce heat and simmer for 20 minutes till vegetables are cooked.
- Season with salt and paprika and stir in oregano. Adjust seasoning as required.
- You can either serve the soup chunky or if you prefer it smooth, blend the soup in a blender and puree to taste.

Serve garnished with bread croutons on the top.

Thick and hearty vegetable and potato soup with a wonderful rich and creamy flavour.

Potatoes – British Cuisine

Preparation time
10 minutes

Cooking time
40 minutes

Serves
4

Cheesy Potato Rosettes

Ingredients

480 g / 16 oz Small potatoes
900 ml Water
1 teaspoon Salt

½ teaspoon White pepper powder
120 g / 4 oz Cheddar cheese
Pinch of nutmeg

60 ml / 2 Fl oz milk

Method

- Wash and place the potatoes in a saucepan, cover with water and bring to boil.
- Simmer potatoes till tender, drain and peel off the skin.
- Mash the potatoes with potato masher, ensuring a smooth texture without lumps.
- Add salt, pepper, nutmeg and milk and mix them well.
- Add cheese and mix well.
- Preheat oven to 200°C / 400°F
- Take a piping bag with a large nozzle and fill it with the potato mixture.
- Oil a baking tray and pipe potato rosettes on the tray.
- Bake in the oven for 20 minutes or until tops of the rosette start to take on a slight colour.

Serve with any vegetable stew.

Oven baked fluffy mashed potato rosettes flavoured with cheese and nutmeg.

Preparation time
10 minutes

Cooking time
20 minutes

Serves
4

Potato and Onion Bake

Ingredients

3 Medium par boiled potatoes

1 Red onion finely diced

60 g / 2 oz Grated cheddar cheese

½ teaspoon Salt

½ teaspoon Pepper

1 tablespoon Olive oil

Method

- Slice the par boiled potatoes into 5 mm thick slices.
- Oil 4 individual ramekin dishes.
- Line the bottom of each ramekin dish with potato slices. Overlap the potato slices so that the base of the ramekin is well covered.
- Season the potato layer with salt and pepper and add a layer of diced onions.
- Add another layer of potato slices and season with salt and pepper and add another layer of onions.
- Add a final layer of potato slices and season with salt and pepper.
- Finish the layers with a sprinkling of grated cheddar cheese.
- Bake the potato and cheese bakes in a preheated oven 190°C / 375°F for 20 minutes till cheese starts to bubble and turns brown.
- Remove from oven.

Serve hot with a side salad.

Crispy, cheesy potato and onion bake, a delicious accompaniment to any main course.

Preparation time
15 minutes

Cooking time
40 minutes

Serves
2

Griddled Potatoes

Ingredients

6 Medium potatoes
1 teaspoon Salt
Spray cooking oil

For garnish:
1 teaspoon Chilli flakes
½ teaspoon Salt

For Chilli Tamarind dip:
4 tablespoons Tamarind pulp
1 tablespoon Brown sugar
4 Ripe stoned dates
1 teaspoon Chilli powder
½ teaspoon Salt
½ tablespoon Chopped fresh coriander

Method

Chilli and Tamarind Dip:
- Place the tamarind pulp, brown sugar, dates, chilli powder and salt into a blender and blend them to form a smooth paste. Transfer to a serving dish and stir in the fresh coriander.

Griddled Potatoes:
- Place the potatoes in large pan of water and add salt.
- Boil the potatoes till they are ¾ cooked.
- Remove the potatoes from the water and peel them.
- Slice the potatoes into slices approximately 5 mm thick.
- Heat a griddle pan and spray it with cooking oil.
- Lay in small batches the slices of precooked potatoes on the griddle pan and cook till brown spots and brown lines appear on the potato slices.
- Turn the potato slices to cook both sides.
- Transfer the potato slices to a baking tray and cover with foil to keep them warm.
- Repeat for remaining potato slices.
- Garnish the griddled potatoes with salt and chilli flakes and serve with Chilli and Tamarind dip.

Crispy potato bites, simple but delicious with a tangy chilli and tamarind dip.

Preparation time
5 minutes

Cooking time
30 minutes

Serves
2

Jacket Potato with Cheese and Baked Beans

Ingredients

2 Large baking potatoes

Salt and pepper to taste

30 g / 1 oz Cheddar cheese grated

60 g / 2 oz Baked beans in tomato sauce

2 teaspoons Butter

Method

- Wash the potatoes, and prick them with a fork.
- Preheat oven to 200°C / 400°F.
- Place the potatoes on a baking tray in the oven and bake for 30 minutes till they are cooked inside and the skin is crispy. (You may need to rotate the potatoes half way through the cooking time.)
- Remove potatoes from the oven and place them on a serving dish. Cut a cross on top of each baked potato and fluff up the inside of the potato with a fork. Add a teaspoon of butter and season with salt and pepper.
- Heat the baked beans for 2-3 minutes and pour them over the baked potatoes.
- Sprinkle with grated cheddar and serve immediately with a side salad.

An oven baked potato, light and fluffy inside with a crispy outer skin, filled with delicious baked beans and garnished with grated cheddar cheese.

Potatoes – British Cuisine | 31

Preparation time
10 minutes

Cooking time
20 minutes

Serves
2

Diced Sweet Potato Bites

Ingredients

2 Large sweet potatoes

900 ml Sunflower oil

½ teaspoon Salt

½ teaspoon Pepper

Method

- Wash and peel the sweet potatoes and cut them into 1 cm cubes.
- Heat oil in a deep pan and when it is hot, fry the sweet potato in batches till they turn golden brown and crispy.
- Remove them from oil and drain the potato bites on kitchen paper.
- Transfer to serving dish and sprinkle with salt and pepper.

Serve hot with sour cream and chilli dip.

Decadent and crispy sweet potato bites that will leave you wanting more and more.

Preparation time
10 minutes

Cooking time
20 minutes

Serves
4

Sweet Potato Mash

Ingredients

- 1 Large sweet potato
- 30 g / 1 oz Butter
- 60 ml Cream
- Pinch of salt and black pepper
- ½ teaspoon Nutmeg

Method

- Cut the sweet potato into chunks and boil it until tender.
- Place the sweet potato in a bowl and mash it with a fork until it is smooth.
- Add butter, cream, nutmeg, salt and pepper and mix well.
- Transfer to a serving dish.

Serve as a side dish or as an accompaniment to a main course.

Creamy rich sweet potato gently flavoured with nutmeg.

Preparation time
30 minutes

Cooking time
25 minutes

Makes
14 scones

Serves
7

Sweet Potato Scones

Ingredients

360 g / 12 oz Plain flour
90 g / 3 oz Brown sugar
30 g / 1 oz Brown sugar for sprinkling on scones

2 ½ teaspoons Baking powder
½ teaspoon Salt
120 g / 4 oz Chilled butter

180 g / 6 oz Cooked sweet potato puree
¼ teaspoon Cinnamon powder
75 ml Butter milk

Method

- In a bowl, sieve the flour and baking powder and keep them aside.
- Add butter to the flour and rub it with light fingers to form a bread crumb type mixture.
- Add 90 g sugar and mix it using a fork.
- Add sweet potato puree and mix it into the flour. Add small amounts of butter milk at a time and mix until mixture comes together but it is not sticky.
- Transfer the mixture to a floured surface and roll out the dough in a round circle to approx 2.5 cm thickness.

- Using a cookie cutter cut out round scones and place them on a greased baking tray.
- Roll up the remaining dough and repeat till all the dough is used up.
- Sprinkle the scones with reserved sugar and bake the scones in preheated oven 175˚C / 350˚F for approx 25-30 minutes or until scones turn a golden brown colour.
- Remove from oven and cool scones on a wire rack.

Serve them with jam and clotted cream.

Sweet and deliciously fragranced scones delicately flavoured with sweet potato and cinnamon.

34 | Potatoes – American Cuisine

Preparation time
20 minutes

Cooking time
20 minutes

Chilling time
30 minutes

Serves
4

Potato and Courgette Fritters

Ingredients

3 Medium par boiled potatoes
1 Medium courgette / zucchini
1 Green chilli finely chopped
1½ teaspoons Salt
1 teaspoon Black pepper
½ teaspoon Chilli flakes
1 tablespoon Chick pea flour
1 tablespoon Rice flour
1 tablespoon Plain flour for dusting
90 ml Sunflower oil for shallow frying
3 tablespoons Sweet red chilli sauce for serving

Method

- In a bowl mix together salt, pepper, chickpea flour, rice flour and chilli flakes.
- Grate the courgette with the skin on and add it to the flour mix with green chilli and combine them well.
- Grate the potatoes and stir them into the courgette and flour mixture with light hands.
- In a shallow tray place the plain flour.
- Divide the potato and courgette mixture into 8 parts and gently pat each portion to form a small round cake shape.
- Dust the cake with plain flour and shake off the excess.
- Place the potato fritters on a tray and chill for 30 minutes.
- Heat oil in a frying pan and shallow fry the potato and courgette fritters on medium heat till golden brown on both sides. Remove from pan and place on kitchen paper to drain access oil.

Transfer to serving dish and serve with sweet red chilli sauce.

Delectable and tasty snacks with a crispy outer coating for a savoury bite.

Preparation time	Cooking time	Serves
10 minutes	60 minutes	4

Aubergine and Potato Bake

Ingredients

1 Large Dutch aubergine
3 Medium par boiled potatoes
1 teaspoon Salt
60 g / 2 oz Feta cheese

For sauce:
4 Large tomatoes finely chopped
1 Large tablespoon tomato puree
1 Red onion

1 Large courgette finely diced
1 teaspoon Salt
1 teaspoon Black pepper
½ teaspoon Chopped garlic

3 tablespoons Olive oil
1 teaspoon Salt
1 teaspoon Sugar

Method

- Remove the stalk and slice the aubergine length ways into paper thin slices, sprinkle the slices with salt and place them in a colander to remove bitter juices.
- Heat olive oil in a pan and when it is hot add garlic and onions and sauté until onions are translucent. Add the courgettes and sauté for 5 more minutes till courgettes are cooked.
- Add chopped tomatoes, tomato puree and sugar. Simmer them on low heat and cook the sauce till tomatoes break down and the sauce thickens. Season with salt and pepper.
- Slice the potatoes into 5 mm thick slices.
- Grease a large oven proof pie dish with oil.
- Pat dry the aubergine slices to remove any excess moisture. In a pan add a little oil and shallow fry the aubergine slices in small batches until soft and they turn brown coloured on both sides. Drain on kitchen paper.
- Line the bottom of the pie dish with half the aubergine slices.
- Cover the slices with some of the tomato sauce.
- Arrange a layer of potato slices on top of the tomato sauce.
- Add some tomato sauce on top of the potato slices and add another layer of aubergine slices.
- Add one final layer of tomato sauce and crumble the feta cheese on top of the sauce. Finish with a layer of potato slices on top of the cheese.
- Brush the final layer of potato slices with a little oil and bake in a preheated over at 175°C / 375°F for 45 minutes until potatoes slices start to brown and crisp up.

Remove from oven and allow it to cool slightly. Serve with a fresh garden salad.

A delicious and healthy bake with a medley of flavours.

Preparation time
20 minutes

Cooking time
30 minutes

Chilling time
30 minutes

Serves
4

Potato and Spinach Balls

Ingredients

180 g / 6 oz Boiled potatoes
90 g / 3 oz Cooked spinach puree
½ teaspoon Salt
½ teaspoon Chilli powder
¼ teaspoon Cinnamon powder
¼ teaspoon Clove powder
1 tablespoon Lemon juice
1 tablespoon Corn flour
2 tablespoons Bread crumbs
¼ teaspoon Bicarbonate of soda
200 ml Sunflower oil

Method

- In a bowl add potatoes, salt, chilli powder, bicarbonate of soda, cinnamon, clove powder and lemon juice. Mix them well.
- Squeeze the spinach to remove excess water and add the spinach to the potato mixture.
- Add corn flour and bread crumbs to the bowl and mix together to form a firm mixture.
- Dust hands with corn flour and pinch walnut sized balls of the mixture and roll them into balls.
- Place all the balls on an oiled tray and chill for 30 minutes.
- Heat oil in a frying pan, when it is hot shallow fry the potato and spinach balls in batches till they turn golden brown and crispy.
- Drain on kitchen paper to remove excess oil.

Transfer to a serving dish and serve with sweet chilli sauce.

Crispy coated potato and spinach balls with a spicy kick in every bite.

Potatoes – Greek Cuisine

Preparation time
10 minutes

Cooking time
20 minutes

Serves
2

Potato and Lentil Burritos

Ingredients

4 Tortilla wraps
240 g / 8 oz Precooked green lentils
120 g / 4 oz Precooked aduki beans
1 Large potato peeled and grated
1 Red onion finely chopped
1 ½ teaspoons Salt

2 Cloves garlic finely minced
2 tablespoons Tomato puree
1 tablespoon Tomato ketchup
1 ½ tablespoons Hot chilli sauce
1 tablespoon Chopped parsley
2 tablespoons Olive oil

For garnish:
1 Medium tomato deseeded and finely diced
1 tablespoon Red capsicum finely diced
1 tablespoon Green capsicum finely diced
60 g / 2 oz Grated cheddar cheese

Method

- Heat oil in a pan. When it is hot add garlic and onions and sauté till onions are soft and translucent.
- Add potatoes and sauté for 5 minutes until they are tender and cooked.
- Add beans and lentils followed by tomato puree, tomato ketchup, chilli sauce and salt.
- Add 60 ml water and cook the mixture till it thickens.
- Stir in chopped parsley.
- In a griddle warm the burrito wrap, once it is warm transfer it to a serving dish.
- Spoon the potato and lentil mixture in the centre of the burrito and top it with chopped tomatoes and red and green capsicums.
- Sprinkle with grated cheese and wrap the burrito in a roll.
- Cut in half and serve immediately.
- Alternatively prepare all four burritos in this way, place them side by side on a baking tray and sprinkle with extra cheese.
- Place the prepared and filled burritos under a preheated grill till cheese bubbles and melts.

Serve hot with a side salad.

Mexican style burritos with a spicy lentil, bean and potato filling.

Preparation time
10 minutes

Cooking time
30 minutes

Serves
4

Potato and Mixed Bean Pate

Ingredients

240 g / 8 oz Precooked mixed beans (bortolli/ aduki/haricot)
1 Medium boiled potato
1 tablespoon Fresh chopped coriander leaves
1 Clove of garlic
1 Green chilli

2 tablespoons Mixed finely diced peppers
1 Small shallot finely diced
1 tablespoon Lemon juice
½ teaspoon Salt
½ teaspoon White pepper powder
1 tablespoon Olive oil

1 tablespoon White wine vinegar
¼ teaspoon Chilli flakes

For Serving:
1 packet Crackers/ Tortilla chips/ Melba toast

Method

- Put the beans, potato, coriander leaves, green chilli, garlic, salt, pepper, lemon juice, olive oil, vinegar and chilli flakes into a blender jug and grind the mixture to form a smooth pate.
- Transfer mixture to a bowl and stir in the finely diced peppers and shallots.
- Mix well and transfer it to a serving dish. Chill for 30 minutes.

Serve the pate with crackers / tortilla chips or Melba toast.

Creamy and rich bean pate delicately spiced and flavoured with herbs.

Preparation time

20 minutes

Cooking time

5 minutes

Serves

2

Potato and Bean Tacos

Ingredients

Filling:
2 Medium boiled potatoes diced
120 g / 4 oz pre cooked borlotti beans
1 Small onion finely chopped
1 Small clove garlic finely minced
1 teaspoon Salt
½ teaspoon Cumin powder
1 Red chilli finely chopped
½ teaspoon Paprika powder
1 teaspoon Tomato puree
1 tablespoon Olive oil
4 Taco corn shells

Topping:
60 g / 2 oz Grated cheddar cheese
1 Bowl mixed salad; lettuce, cucumber, carrots, tomato, peppers, red onion

Method

- In a frying pan add the oil when it is hot sauté the garlic and then add the onions and cook till they turn soft and translucent.
- Add the salt, chilli, paprika and cumin powders and sauté for 1 more minute.
- Add the pre cooked bortolli beans and 60 ml water and tomato puree. Cook the mixture for 2-3 minutes. Using the back of a spoon, mash the beans slightly to break them down.
- Add the diced potato and cook the mixture till all the water evaporates. Filling should be dry.
- Place the tacos under a preheated grill for 1 minute to warm them.
- Remove from grill and wrap each taco in a paper napkin. Spoon into the taco shell the potato and bean filling, top it with the mixed salad followed by the grated cheese.

Serve immediately.

Crispy crunchy corn shell filled with a spicy potato and bean filling topped with a generous salad and cheese topping.

Potatoes – Mexican Cuisine | 41

Preparation time
20 minutes

Cooking time
15 minutes

Serves
4

Savoury Potato Biscuits

Ingredients

240 g / 8 oz All purpose flour

2 Small potatoes boiled and mashed

½ tablespoon Red chilly flakes

1 teaspoon Baking powder

½ teaspoon Freshly grounded black pepper

¾ teaspoon Salt

2 teaspoons Olive oil

Method

- In a bowl add flour, salt, pepper, chilli flakes and baking powder. Mix all the spices with the flour.
- Add mashed potato and olive oil and make a firm dough, the liquid from the potato will determine if you need to add any extra water to make the dough.
- On a floured surface roll out the dough and using cookie cutters cut out biscuits and place on a well oiled baking tray.
- Bake in a preheated oven at 175°C/ 375°F for approx 12-15 minutes.
- Biscuits are ready when they turn golden brown.

Serve these warm with a chive and yoghurt dip.

Crunchy, little mini bites that are moreish and simply delectable.

Preparation time
20 minutes

Cooking time
40 minutes

Serves
4

Baked Tortilla Wraps

Ingredients

- 4 Tortilla wraps
- 4 Medium boiled potatoes
- 120 g / 4 oz Grated mozzarella cheese
- 100 ml Sunflower oil
- ½ teaspoon Salt
- ½ teaspoon Paprika powder

Salsa sauce:
- 4 Medium tomatoes deseeded and finely chopped
- 1 Small red onion finely diced
- 30 g / 1 oz Green peppers finely chopped
- 1 teaspoon Dried oregano
- 1 teaspoon Salt
- 1 teaspoon Sugar
- ½ teaspoon Cumin powder
- 1 tablespoon Olive oil
- ½ teaspoon Garlic paste
- ½ teaspoon Paprika powder

Method

- Slice the potatoes into 5 mm thick slices and shallow fry them in batches in sunflower oil till they turn golden brown and are crispy. Drain on kitchen paper and sprinkle some salt and paprika powder on it.
- In a pan add olive oil. When it is hot, add garlic and onions and sauté till onions turn translucent.
- Add peppers and diced tomatoes and cook the mixture till tomatoes break down and soften.
- Add cumin, paprika powder, salt and oregano and simmer the sauce until it thickens.
- Line a baking tray with foil and place the tortilla wrap on it.
- Spread the prepared tomato sauce on one half of the tortilla and place 5-6 slices of fried potatoes on top of the sauce.
- Spread a little more sauce on top of the potato slices and sprinkle some cheese on top and fold the tortilla wrap in half to form a semi circle.
- Repeat for the remaining tortilla wraps.
- Place all four wraps on the baking tray and bake in a preheated oven 175°C / 350°F for 20 minutes until wraps crisp up and cheese has melted.
- Remove wraps from oven and cut them into wedges.

Serve hot with remaining Salsa sauce.

Tortillas with crispy potato slices oven baked in a spicy salsa and cheese melt.

Preparation time
10 minutes

Cooking time
15 minutes

Serves
4

Sweet Potato and Mixed Bean Stir Fry

Ingredients

1 Boiled sweet potato diced
1 Tomato
360 g / 12 oz Precooked mixed beans (red kidney beans/ black eyed beans/bortolli and haricot beans/aduki beans)
2 tablespoons Olive oil
½ teaspoon Grounded cumin powder
½ teaspoon Paprika powder
½ teaspoon Salt
1 Green pepper
1 Red pepper

Method

- Place both the peppers under a hot grill to char them, keep turning them to ensure even browning.
- Once peppers are charred remove the skin and dice them into small pieces and place them in a bowl.
- Heat oil in a pan and when it is hot, add diced potatoes and stir fry until potatoes brown slightly, add the mixed beans and stir fry for 2-3 minutes to warm them through.
- Add diced peppers, salt, paprika and cumin powder and toss the potato and bean mixture to coat with the spices. Stir fry for 2-3 minutes longer.
- Cut the tomato in half and remove the seeds. Dice it into small pieces and add to the pan. Toss well. Transfer to a serving dish.

Serve with fresh tortilla wraps.

Sweet potato with smoky grilled peppers and mixed bean stir fry.

44 | Potatoes – Mexican Cuisine

Preparation time
20 minutes

Cooking time
10 minutes

Resting time
20 minutes

Serves
2

Gado Gado Salad

Ingredients

2 Potatoes par boiled
1 Medium carrot
120 g / 4 oz White cabbage thinly shredded
120 g / 4 oz Red cabbage thinly shredded

6 inch Piece of cucumber
1 tablespoon Roasted peanuts
1 teaspoon Toasted sesame seeds
1 tablespoon Sunflower oil

Dressing:
1 tablespoon Dark soya sauce
1 tablespoon Honey
2 tablespoons Lemon juice
1 tablespoon White wine vinegar

1 teaspoon Finely chopped garlic
1 teaspoon Finely chopped ginger
½ teaspoon Chilli flakes
1 tablespoon Piri piri chilli sauce
1 teaspoon Toasted sesame seeds
1 Red chilli cut into thin slices

Method

- Slice the par boiled potatoes into 5 mm thick slices. Heat a griddle and brush it with a little oil.
- Place the potato slices on the hot griddle till they are slightly brown and crisp. Brush the top of the potato slices with remaining oil and turn them over to brown.
- Remove the potato slices from the griddle and place them in a bowl.
- Peel and slice the carrot thinly, add it to the bowl.
- Cut the cucumber in half and remove the seeds using a teaspoon. Slice the cucumber into 5 mm thick slices. Add to the bowl.
- Add red and white cabbage and sliced chilli to the bowl.
- In a pan add honey, lemon juice, vinegar and soya sauce, chilli sauce, garlic, ginger and chilli flakes. Heat the mixture for 1 minute to warm the dressing. Take off the heat and add the toasted sesame seeds.
- Pour the dressing over the salad and toss it well so that all the vegetables are coated in the dressing.
- Leave the salad covered for 15- 20 minutes for flavours to infuse.
- Transfer salad to a serving dish, and garnish with roasted peanuts and remaining sesame seeds.

Serve with noodles.

Fragrant oriental salad with a fusion of flavours.

Preparation time
20 minutes

Cooking time
40 minutes

Serves
2

Stuffed Tomatoes

Ingredients

4 Large firm tomatoes
Filling:
1 Large potato peeled and diced
1 Large carrot grated
120 g / 4 oz Frozen or fresh green peas
1 Handful baby spinach leaves
1 Red onion finely chopped
1 teaspoon Garlic paste
½ teaspoon Salt
½ teaspoon Black pepper
2 tablespoons Tomato ketchup
2 tablespoons Sweet garlic and chilli sauce
2 tablespoons Dark soya sauce
1 tablespoon Lemon juice
2 tablespoons Olive oil
2 tablespoons Roasted salted peanuts

Method

- Grind the peas coarsely and keep them aside.
- Heat oil in a frying pan and when it is hot, add garlic and onions and sauté till onions turn translucent and soft.
- Add peas, carrots, potatoes and 60 ml water. Cover and cook the vegetables approximately for 5-8 minutes, until they are soft and tender.
- Chop the spinach and add to the vegetable mixture, sauté for 2-3 minutes more till spinach leaves wilt.
- Add chilli sauce, tomato sauce and soya sauce, salt and pepper and stir.
- Coarsely grind the salted peanuts and add to the cooked mixture.

Assembling:
- Slice the tops off the tomatoes and scoop out the pulp and seeds using a teaspoon.
- Place the tomatoes on an oiled baking tray.
- Spoon the cooked filling generously into the hollowed out tomatoes.
- Bake the filled tomatoes in a pre heated oven 175°C / 350°F for 10-12 minutes until tomatoes soften slightly but still retain their shape.

Serve hot on a bed of the remaining filling.

Succulent tomatoes filled with a delicious, sweet and tangy vegetable filling.

Preparation time
15 minutes

Cooking time
20 minutes

Serves
4

Sambal Goreng Kentang (Spicy Fried Potatoes)

Ingredients

4 Medium potatoes
1 Medium onion finely diced
1 tablespoon Garlic paste
½ tablespoon Kepak manis (Indonesian sweet soya sauce)
1 tablespoon Sambal oelek (Indonesian chilli sauce)
1 teaspoon Salt
½ teaspoon Chilli powder
1 tablespoon Sunflower oil for cooking
900 ml Sunflower oil for deep frying

Method

- Peel and slice the potatoes into thin round slices.
- Heat oil in a deep pan, when it is hot deep fry the potato slices in batches until they turn golden brown.
- Drain on kitchen paper.
- In a pan, add sunflower oil and sauté the garlic and onions until they turn translucent.
- Add Kepak Manis, Sambal Oelek, salt and chilli powder and sauté for 1 more minute.
- Add fried potatoes and toss them well in the sauce.
- Transfer to a serving dish and garnish with finely sliced sweet peppers.

Crispy fried potatoes stir fried in pungent and spicy Indonesian flavours.

Preparation time
20 minutes

Cooking time
30 minutes

Chilling time
30 minutes

Serves
4

Sesame Coins

Ingredients

- 2 Medium boiled potatoes
- 1 teaspoon Salt
- ½ teaspoon Cumin powder
- ½ teaspoon Chilli powder
- 1 tablespoon Lemon juice
- ½ teaspoon Garam masala
- 1 tablespoon Freshly chopped coriander
- 6 Slices of bread
- 3 tablespoons Sunflower oil
- 1 Tablespoon Sesame seeds
- 3 tablespoons Milk

NB- Garam masala- coriander seeds, cumin seeds, black pepper corns, black cumin seeds, dry ginger powder, cardamom, cloves and cinnamon.

Method

- In a bowl, add boiled potatoes and mash them with a potato masher.
- Add salt, chilli powder, garam masala, cumin, lemon juice and coriander and mix them well into the potato mixture.
- Divide the mixture into 12 balls and flatten each one to form a round 2.5 cm disc. Keep them aside.
- Remove the crusts from the bread and using a cookie cutter cut out 2 circles each 2.5 cm round from each bread slice.
- Brush the top of each bread circle with a little milk and place the potato discs on top of the bread. Press together with the palms of your hand to make the potato stick to the bread slice.
- Place the sesame seeds in a dish. Dip the bread potato side down into some milk and then into the sesame seeds so that they stick to the side with the potato mixture. Press with the palms of your hand to make the sesame seeds stick to the potato side. Repeat for remaining bread circles.
- Place sesame coins on an oiled tray and chill for half an hour.
- Heat a frying pan with some oil. Shallow fry sesame coins in batches of 4 until they turn golden brown on both sides. Transfer to kitchen paper to drain any excess oil.

Serve hot with Tomato ketchup.

Crispy Sesame coated potato coins with a spicy bite.

Preparation time
10 minutes

Cooking time
15 minutes

Serves
4

Bread Appetizers

Ingredients

12 Thin slices of wholemeal bread
2 Large boiled potatoes diced
240 g / 8 oz Boiled white chickpeas
3 tablespoons of Mixed red, yellow and green peppers finely diced
1 Red onion finely diced
2 tablespoons Lemon juice
1 teaspoon Salt
½ teaspoon Red chilli powder
2 tablespoons Olive oil
1 tablespoon Freshly chopped coriander

Method

- Remove the crusts from the bread slices and cut the slices into round circles approx 12 cm in diameter or as large as the bread slice will allow.
- Spray a muffin tray with some oil and push the bread circles into each hole to line it.
- Bake the bread cases in a pre heated oven 200°C / 400°F for about 10-12 minutes till the bread cases start to turn crisp and golden brown.
- In a pan, heat the olive oil and when it is hot, add boiled diced potatoes and chick peas to it and stir fry till they are warmed through.
- Season with salt and chilli powder and add lemon juice.
- Add peppers, onions and coriander and toss them together.
- Spoon the filling into the pre baked bread cases and serve immediately.

A fast and speedy appetizer that is perfect as a party dish.

Potatoes – Asian Fusion Cuisine

Preparation time	Cooking time	Serves
20 minutes	50 minutes	2

Spicy Potato Nests

Ingredients

480 g / 16 oz Potatoes

1 teaspoon Salt

60 g / 2 oz Grated cheddar cheese

30 ml Milk

Filling:

1 Courgette finely diced

1 Red onion finely diced

1 teaspoon Garlic paste

3 tablespoons Red, green and yellow finely diced capsicums

2 Button mushrooms finely diced

120 g / 4 oz Cherry tomatoes

375 ml Sieved tomatoes

8 Basil leaves

1 tablespoon Dry oregano

2 Green chillies finely chopped

1 teaspoon Sugar

1 teaspoon Salt

½ teaspoon Freshly grounded black pepper

2 tablespoons Olive oil

Method

- Boil the potatoes in 900 ml water for 20 minutes until tender.
- Remove the skin from the potatoes and mash them while still hot.
- Add salt, pepper, milk and cheese and mix well to form a rich creamy lump free mash potato.
- Grease a baking tray with some oil.
- Fill a piping bag with a large nozzle with the mashed potato mixture.
- Pipe four 3 inch round swirls approximately 2 inches high onto the oiled baking tray.
- Using a teaspoon slightly hollow out the centre by pushing the potato to the sides to make room to fill the nests with the filling later.
- Bake for 15 minutes in a pre heated oven at 175°C / 350°F till slightly golden brown.

Filling:

- Heat oil in a pan, when its hot sauté garlic and onions till they are translucent and soft.
- Add courgette, peppers, mushrooms and sauté for further 5 minutes till the vegetables soften and they are completely cooked.
- Add sieved tomatoes and the chillies, salt, pepper, sugar and oregano and simmer sauce for 7-8 minutes until it starts to thicken.
- Cut half the cherry tomatoes and tear the basil leaves and stir them both into the sauce.
- Simmer the sauce for another 7-8 minutes till the tomatoes soften and basil leaves wilt.

To assemble:

- Remove potato nests from oven and if necessary push the centre down with a teaspoon to create a cavity. Spoon a generous amount of filling in the centre of each nest and return the filled nests back into the oven for 10 minutes.

Serve piping hot with a side salad.

Oven baked creamy potato nests filled with an aromatic spicy Italian tomato filling.

Preparation time
20 minutes

Cooking time
40 minutes

Chilling time
30 minutes

Serves
4

Spicy Potato Croquettes

Ingredients

3 Medium potatoes

1 teaspoon Chilli powder

1 teaspoon Salt

120 g / 4 oz Bread crumbs

120 ml Sunflower oil

1 Egg

Method

- Boil the potatoes for 15-20 minutes until tender.
- Peel the skin off the potatoes and mash them ensuring there are no lumps.
- Add salt and chilli powder and mix well.
- Divide the potato mixture into walnut sized balls.
- Beat the egg and pour it into a shallow dish.
- Place the bread crumbs into a shallow dish.
- Take each potato ball and roll it into a 2 cm cylindrical sausage shape, dip it into the beaten egg and then roll into the bread crumbs to coat evenly all over. Repeat for all the potato balls.
- Place them on a tray and chill for 30 minutes.
- Heat oil in a frying pan and when it is hot, shallow fry the potato croquettes till they turn golden brown. Drain on kitchen paper to remove any excess oil.
- Transfer to a serving dish.

Serve hot with Chilli dip.

Light spicy bites that are perfect as a party appetizer or for nibbling.

52 | Potatoes – Asian Fusion Cuisine

Preparation time
20 minutes

Cooking time
20 minutes

Serves
4

Potato and Lentil Pancakes

Ingredients

- 60 g / 2 oz Boiled moong beans
- 60 g / 2 oz Boiled split chick peas (dhal)
- 2 Medium par boiled potatoes
- 1 tablespoon Chopped fresh coriander leaves
- ½ teaspoon Salt
- 2 Green chillies finely chopped
- ½ teaspoon Fresh ginger paste
- ¼ teaspoon Bicarbonate of soda
- 60 ml / 2 fl oz sunflower oil for shallow frying
- ¼ teaspoon White pepper powder
- 1 tablespoon Lemon juice

Method

- Drain the moong beans and boiled split chickpeas to remove any extra cooking liquid. Put them into a large bowl.
- Add coriander leaves, chillies, ginger, salt, bicarbonate of soda, pepper and lemon juice and mix them well.
- Grate the par boiled potatoes and gently fold them into the lentil mixture.
- Heat a shallow frying pan with a little oil and drop spoonfuls of the mixture, gently patting it down to form pancakes approx 3 inches in diameter.
- Cook for 1-2 minutes and flip them over to cook top once the underside is golden brown. Add a little more oil if needed. Cook on medium heat till pancakes are golden brown on both the sides.
- Remove the cooked pancakes and keep them warm and repeat for the remaining mixture.
- Transfer pancakes to the serving dish.

Serve with yoghurt chutney or dipping sauce of choice.

Protein packed pancakes perfect for picnics and lunch boxes.

Potatoes – Asian Fusion Cuisine | 53

Preparation time	Cooking time	Serves
40 minutes	45 minutes	6

Spring Rolls

Ingredients

1 Packet chinese spring roll pastry sheets (or phyllo pastry)
2 Medium potatoes peeled and cut into fine strips (julienne)
120 g / 4 oz Bean sprouts
1 Large red onion sliced into thin strips
120 g / 4 oz Carrots cut into fine thin strips (julienne)
1 Each red, green, yellow capsicum cut into very thin strips
2 teaspoons Garlic paste
2 teaspoons Ginger paste
1 teaspoon Salt
2 tablespoons Soya sauce
1 tablespoon Chilli sauce
2 tablespoons Sunflower oil
3 Green chillies finely chopped
900 ml Sunflower oil for deep frying

For paste to stick the edges down:
60 g / 2 oz Plain flour and 4 tablespoons water mixed together to form a thick paste

Method

- Heat oil in a wok and add ginger and garlic.
- Add the onions, peppers, potatoes and carrots and stir fry till tender but crisp.
- Add the salt, chillies, soya sauce and chilli sauce.
- Add the bean sprouts.
- Stir fry again and remove from heat.
- Set aside to cool.

Rolling the spring rolls:

- Separate the sheets of spring roll pastry and place on a flat surface.
- Take a spoon full of vegetable mixture and place it at the bottom edge of pastry in the centre only.
- Start to roll pastry from bottom edge to make 2 folds.
- Fold the right and left sides of pastry to meet in the centre.
- Roll the spring roll again into a tight roll, just before you get to the top edge spread the flour paste and stick the pastry down at the end so that it does not come unstuck when frying.
- Repeat same procedure for rest of the pastry. Keep rolled spring rolls covered with a damp cloth to prevent the pastry from drying out.
- Heat oil in a wok and deep fry spring rolls on medium heat till they turn golden brown.
- Drain on kitchen paper and transfer to serving dish.

Serve with chilli sauce, soya sauce or chutney of your choice for dipping.

Shredded vegetables stir fried and encased in Chinese spring roll pastry. Deep fried to golden brown to make a crispy crunchy Indo Chinese snack.

Preparation time
20 minutes

Cooking time
20 minutes

Serves
1

Potato and Vegetable Stir Fry

Ingredients

2 Medium boiled Potatoes
1 Large Carrot
120 g / 4 oz French beans
1 tablespoon Dark soya sauce

1 tablespoon Chilli sauce
1 tablespoon Lemon juice
1 tablespoon Sesame seeds
1 tablespoon Sunflower Oil

½ tablespoon Sesame Seed Oil
¼ teaspoon Salt

Method

- Slice the potatoes into round slices approx 5mm thick each. Cut the slices into halves.
- Peel and slice the carrot into round circles or decoratively to your choice.
- Cut top and tail of the French beans and boil them in salted water for 5 minutes. After 5 minutes remove them from boiling water and plunge them into a bowl of iced water to refresh them.
- In a wok heat up the sunflower oil and sesame seed oil. When it is hot add the potato slices and stir fry for 2-3 minutes until they start to brown slightly on both sides. Add the carrots, french beans and sesame seeds, stir fry for a further 5 minutes.
- Add the soya sauce, chilli sauce and lemon juice, toss the vegetables until evenly coated.
- Transfer to a serving dish.

Serve with egg fried rice.

Hot spicy vegetable and potatoes sautéed in a spicy sesame oil dressing.

Preparation time
10 minutes

Cooking time
20 minutes

Serves
4

Sweet and Sour Potatoes

Ingredients

3 Large boiled potatoes
½ teaspoon Ginger paste
½ teaspoon Garlic paste
1 tablespoon Sunflower oil
2 Spring onions sliced thinly

For sauce:
75 ml Rice vinegar
60 g / 2 oz brown sugar
1 tablespoon Tomato ketchup
1 teaspoon Soy sauce

2 teaspoons Cornstarch mixed with 4 teaspoons water
½ teaspoon Chilli flakes
½ teaspoon Salt

Method

- In a pan add the vinegar, soya sauce, ketchup, chilli flakes and brown sugar and bring to boil.
- Add the cornstarch mixture to the sauce and simmer on a low heat until the sweet and sour sauce thickens. Remove from heat and keep aside.
- In a wok heat the sunflower oil, when it is hot add the diced potatoes and stir fry to crisp them. Add the garlic and ginger paste and sauté for 1-2 minutes more.
- Add the sweet and sour sauce and toss to coat the potatoes in the sauce. Stir fry until most of the sauce has coated the potatoes.
- Transfer the sweet and sour potatoes to a serving dish and garnish with the chopped spring onions.

Tangy and spicy sweet and sour potatoes delicately flavoured with fusion of garlic and ginger.

Preparation time
20 minutes

Cooking time
20 minutes

Serves
2

Potato and Peas Curry

Ingredients

240 g / 8 oz Peas (fresh or frozen)
2 Medium potatoes peeled and diced
2 Medium tomatoes deseeded and blended to a puree
1 clove of Garlic finely minced

1 teaspoon Salt
1 teaspoon Turmeric powder
1 teaspoon Chilli powder
½ teaspoon Cumin powder
½ teaspoon Coriander powder

1 teaspoon Tomato puree
1 tablespoon Freshly chopped coriander leaves
2 tablespoons Olive oil
100 ml Water
½ teaspoon Mustard seeds

Method

- Heat oil in a pan, when it is hot add mustard seeds and wait for them to splutter.
- Sauté garlic in oil and add blended fresh tomatoes and tomato puree.
- Add salt, turmeric, chilli powder, coriander powder, cumin powder and cook till the tomatoes start to separate from the oil.
- Add the potatoes and peas and water.
- Bring the curry to boil then turn down the heat. Cover and cook till potatoes are fully cooked. (Approx 10 minutes). If you want more gravy then add a little extra water.
- Transfer to a serving dish and garnish with freshly chopped coriander.

Serve with Rice.

A fast and easy classic curry with simple mouth watering flavours.

Preparation time
10 minutes

Cooking time
25 minutes

Resting time
30 minutes

Serves
4

Sweet Potato Pudding

Ingredients

1 Large sweet potato boiled and mashed
1 tablespoon Clarified butter or unsalted butter
1 teaspoon Cardamom powder
½ teaspoon Saffron strands
3 tablespoons Sugar
250 ml Milk
Few almond halves and pinch of saffron for garnishing

Method

- In a heavy bottomed pan add clarified butter, saffron, milk and mashed sweet potato.
- On medium heat, keep stirring the mixture until the milk has reduced and pudding has thickened.
- Add sugar and keep stirring until it melts, take care that the pudding does not stick or scorch.
- Add cardamom powder and stir it in.
- Transfer to serving dishes and garnish with saffron strands and almond halves.

Can be served hot or alternatively serve cold after chilling for 30 minutes.

Creamy and light dessert delicately fragranced with cardamom and saffron.

Preparation time
20 minutes

Cooking time
40 minutes

Marinating time
4 hours

Serves
2

Baby Potatoes in White Gravy

Ingredients

8 Baby potatoes
1 teaspoon Salt
900 ml Water
2 Bay leaves
2 Cardamom pods

1 Red dried chilli
½ teaspoon Mustard seeds
2 tablespoons Sunflower oil
1 tablespoon Freshly chopped coriander

Marinade:
120 g / 4 oz Natural yoghurt
60 g / 2 oz ground cashew nuts
1 teaspoon Ginger paste
1½ teaspoons Chilli paste

1 teaspoon Salt
½ teaspoon Garlic paste

Method

- Wash the potatoes and place them in a large pan with water. Add 1 teaspoon salt and cook for 20 minutes or until tender.
- Peel the skin off the potatoes and prick them with a fork.
- In another bowl, whisk the yoghurt adding the ground cashew nuts, ginger, chillies, garlic and salt.
- Place the pre boiled potatoes in the yoghurt marinade and mix well so that all the potatoes are well coated. Cover and refrigerate for 3-4 hours.

- In a wok, add oil and when it is hot add the mustard seeds and red dried chilli and a couple of bay leaves along with cardamom pods. Wait for the mustard seeds to splutter.
- Add the marinated potatoes and the marinade to hot oil and stir fry for 5 minutes till potatoes are warm throughout. Keep tossing the potatoes otherwise the yoghurt will curdle.
- Transfer to a serving dish and garnish with freshly chopped coriander leaves.

Serve with Vegetable Rice.

Creamy rich gravy coating tender baby potatoes in a fusion of fragrant spices.

Preparation time
10 minutes

Cooking time
20 minutes

Serves
4

Egg and Potato Curry

Ingredients

4 Hard boiled eggs cut into halves
8 Baby potatoes boiled
1 Small red onion finely chopped
½ teaspoon Garlic paste
1 teaspoon Green chilli paste
2 Medium tomatoes blended to a puree

1 teaspoon Salt
½ teaspoon Mustard seeds
2 Red dried chillies
1 teaspoon Turmeric
½ teaspoon Cumin powder
½ teaspoon Coriander powder

½ teaspoon Chilli powder
½ Cup water
2 tablespoons Sunflower oil
2 tablespoons Cream
1 tablespoon Fresh finely chopped coriander

Method

- Heat the oil in a pan. When it is hot add mustard seeds and red chilli and allow them to splutter. Next add the garlic and onions and sauté until onions turn translucent.
- Add blended tomatoes and green chillies, followed by salt, turmeric, cumin and coriander powders and cook for 3-4 minutes till the spices infuse into the tomato and onion mixture and the gravy starts to separate oil.
- Add 3 tablespoons water to the gravy and mix thoroughly.
- Add the boiled egg halves and boiled potatoes and mix gently so that the yolk does not separate from the egg.
- Once the curry is warmed through, stir in the cream. Transfer to a serving dish and garnish with chopped coriander.

Serve with Rice and Naan.

A creamy and rich gravy coating tender baby new potatoes and hard boiled eggs.

Preparation time
10 minutes

Cooking time
20 minutes

Serves
3

Bombay Potatoes

Ingredients

3 Medium potatoes
1 teaspoon Turmeric
1 tablespoon Oil
½ teaspoon Chilli powder
½ teaspoon Coriander powder
½ teaspoon Cumin powder
1 ½ teaspoons Salt
1 tablespoon Tomato puree
½ teaspoon Mustard seeds
1 Red dried chilli
1 tablespoon Fresh coriander finely chopped for garnishing

Method

- Peel and dice the potatoes into 1 inch cubes.
- Heat the oil in a pan and when it is hot, add mustard seeds and red dried chilli. Let them pop.
- Add potatoes followed by salt, turmeric, chilli powder, cumin and coriander powders. Toss the potatoes to evenly coat them with the spices.
- Mix 30 ml water with the tomato puree and add the mixture to the potatoes.
- Toss the potatoes again.
- Cover and cook on a low heat till the potatoes are tender. Approximately for 10-15 minutes. (Intermittently keep tossing the potatoes so that they don't stick to the bottom of the pan.)
- Transfer cooked Bombay potatoes to a serving dish and garnish with fresh coriander.

Serve with rice or Chapatti (Indian flat bread).

Spicy side dish with aromatic flavours of the East.

Index

A
Aubergine and Potato Bake 37

B
Baby Potatoes in White Gravy 60
Baked Tortilla Wraps 43
Bombay Potatoes 62
Bread Appetizers 49

C
Canarian Potatoes 164
Cheesy Potato Rosettes 28

D
Diced Sweet Potato Bites 32

E
Egg and Potato Curry 61

G
Gado Gado Salad 464
Griddled Potatoes 30

H
Hasselback Roast Potatoes 14
Honey Sweet Potatoes 8

J
Jacket Potato with Cheese and Beans 64

L
Lentil and Potato Soup 7

M
Mediterranean Vegetable and Potato Stew 19

N
New Herb Potatoes 18

P
Potato and Bean Tacos 41
Potato and Courgette Fritters 364
Potato and Lentil Burritos 39
Potato and Lentil Pancakes 53
Potato and Mixed Bean Pate 40
Potato and Onion Bake 29
Potato and Peas Curry 58
Potato and Spinach Balls 38
Potato and Vegetable Pie 264
Potato and Vegetable Stir Fry 56
Potato Fries 23
Potato Frittata 16
Potato, Peanut and Sweet Corn Hotpot 64
Potato Sushi Rolls 21

S
Sambal Goreng Kentang (Spicy Fried Potatoes) 47
Savoury Potato Biscuits 42
Sesame Coins 48
Spicy Potato Croquettes 52
Spicy Potato Nests 51
Spring Rolls 564
Stuffed Tomatoes 46
Sweet and Sour Potatoes 57
Sweet Potato and Apple Phyllo Parcels 9
Sweet Potato and Date Halwa 12
Sweet Potato and Mixed Bean Stir Fry 44
Sweet Potato and Red Cabbage Stir Fry 22
Sweet Potato and Tomato Soup 17
Sweet Potato Crisps 26
Sweet Potato Mash 33
Sweet Potato Pudding 59
Sweet Potato Scones 34

V
Vegetable and Potato Soup 27
Vegetable Kebabs 11

POTATOES

First Edition: 2013
1st Impression: 2013

All rights reserved. No part of this book may be reproduced, stored in a retrieval system or transmitted, in any form or by any means, mechanical, photocopying, recording or otherwise, without any prior written permission of the publisher.

© with the author

Published by Kuldeep Jain for

HEALTH HARMONY
An imprint of
B. JAIN PUBLISHERS (P) LTD.
1921/10, Chuna Mandi, Paharganj, New Delhi 110 055 (INDIA)
Tel.: +91-11-4567 1000 • Fax: +91-11-4567 1010
Email: info@bjain.com • Website: www.bjain.com

Printed in India by
JJ Imprints Pvt. Ltd.

ISBN: 978-81-319-1129-7

Weight Conversions

Imperial	Metric	US cups
1 oz	30 gm	
4 oz	120 gm	½ cup
8 oz	240 gm	1 cup
16 oz	480 gm	2 cups

Liquid Conversions

Imperial	Metric	US cups
½ fl oz	15 ml	1 tbsp (level)
1 fl oz	30 ml	
4 fl oz	125 ml	½ cup
8 fl oz	250 ml	1 cup
16 fl oz	500 ml	2 cups
20 fl oz (1 pint)	600 ml	2 ½ cups
33 fl oz (1 litre)		

Oven temperature Conversions

Fahrenheit - °F	Centigrade - °C	Gas
225	110	¼
250	120	½
275	140	1
300	150	2
325	160	3
350	175	4
375	190	5
400	200	6
425	220	7
450	230	8
475	240	9
500	260	10

Notes

All cooking times given in the book are approximate; they may vary slightly with different types of cookers, grills, hobs and microwaves used.

Ratio of water given in making rice and dough can vary depending on different brands used. Water measurements are approximate and a minor adjustment in quantity used may be required.